NIGHTMARE CREATURES SPIDERS!

ORB-WEAVER SPIDERS

Joanne Randolph

PowerKiDS press™

New York

Published in 2014 by The Rosen Publishing Group, Inc.
29 East 21st Street, New York, NY 10010

First Edition

Editor: Jennifer Way and Norman D. Graubart
Book Design: Andrew Povolny
Photo Research: Katie Stryker

Photo Credits: Cover BHJ/Shutterstock.com; p. 5 Michael Lustbader/Photo Researchers/Getty Images; p. 6 Ron Rowan Photography/Shutterstock.com; p. 7 Jon Beard/Shutterstock.com; p. 9 Pan Xunbin/Shutterstock.com; p. 10 Anders Blomqvist/Lonely Planet Images/Getty Images; p. 11 Paul Bertner/Flickr/Getty Images; pp. 12–13 Brandon Blinkenberg/ Shutterstock.com; pp. 14–15, 16 BLANCHOT Philippe/Hermis.fr/Getty Images; p. 17 Charles O. Slavens/Peter Arnold/ Getty Images; p. 18 Paul Baggaley/Flickr/Getty Images; p. 19 (top) Kyu Oh/E+/Getty Images; p. 19 (bottom) Laszlo Podor Photography/Flickr/Getty Images; p. 20 Richard Fellinger/Picture Press/Getty Images; p. 21 Henrik Larsson/ Shutterstock.com; p. 22 Jason Edwards/NATIONAL GEOGRAPHIC IMAGE COLLECTION/Getty Images.

Library of Congress Cataloging-in-Publication Data

Randolph, Joanne.
  Orb-weaver spiders / by Joanne Randolph. — First edition.
     pages cm. — (Nightmare creatures: spiders!)
  ISBN 978-1-4777-2893-2 (library) — ISBN 978-1-4777-2982-3 (pbk.) —
ISBN 978-1-4777-3052-2 (6-pack)
  1. Orb-weavers—Juvenile literature. I. Title.
  QL458.42.A7R36 2014
  595.4'4—dc23
                          2013027036

Manufactured in the United States of America

CPSIA Compliance Information: Batch #W14PK6: For Further Information contact Rosen Publishing, New York, New York at 1-800-237-9932

CONTENTS

MEET THE ORB-WEAVER SPIDER

When people think of spiders, they often picture one sitting in the center of a wheel-shaped web. If you are picturing a spider like this, you are picturing an **orb** weaver! Orb-weaver spiders make some of the most beautiful webs of all spiders. An orb is a circular, ball-like shape. Orb weavers get their name from the round shape of their webs. The scientific name for the orb-weaver family is Araneidae.

There are lots of orb weavers in the world. Some of them are extremely small, and others are some of the largest spiders in the world. In fact, orb-weaving spiders make up about one-fourth of all spider **species**.

This orb-weaver spider is in its web in the Amazon rain forest, in South America. With 3,500 species, orb weavers are one of the largest spider groups.

HOME, WEBBY HOME

Orb weavers live everywhere on Earth except the polar regions. They are often found in backyards, gardens, and forests. They will live anywhere there are lots of bugs to catch and places to spin their webs. They tend to make their homes in wet climates more often than dry ones, but some orb weavers live in dry places like deserts, too.

The branches and leaves of trees provide good places for orb-weaver spiders to build their webs.

This orange orb-weaver spider lives among leaves on a forest floor. Orb-weaver spiders like living in areas where they can blend in with their surroundings.

Orb weavers build their webs in spots where they are likely to catch bugs. Then they usually stay there. They might decide to move if their webs get disturbed a lot, but otherwise they just keep rebuilding their webs in the same places!

ORB-WEAVER BODIES

Orb-weaver spiders, like all spiders, are **arachnids**. As do all arachnids, they have eight legs and two main body parts. The front part is the head. The larger, back part is called the **abdomen**. There are also smaller parts near their mouths called **pedipalps**. The pedipalps are used in **mating**. They look almost like small legs.

Orb weavers have eight small eyes on their heads. Their vision is not great, though. They count on feeling movements in the web more than they do on eyesight. Orb-weaver species can look quite different from one another. Some have smooth, large abdomens. Other species have spikes or bright colors. Still others are dull gray or brown.

Spiny-backed orb-weaver spiders have spines on their abdomens. The spines can be many shapes, sizes, and colors.

AMAZING WEBS

All spiders have special parts called **spinnerets**.
These parts at the back of the abdomen produce silk.
Orb weavers use the spinnerets to build their beautiful,
spiral-shaped webs. They also have three claws on
their feet to help them build the webs.

Golden orb-weaver spiders are sometimes
called writing spiders because of the zigzag
patterns they make in their webs.

This orb-weaver spider is releasing silk from its spinneret. Orb-weaver spiders' silk is light, strong, and stretchy.

The orb weaver starts the web by floating a line of silk on the wind until it sticks to something. Then it fixes the other end to what it is standing on and drops another line from the center to make a Y shape. The spider then builds many arms of silk that are not sticky. It finishes the web by adding a spiral of sticky silk from the center of the web out to the edges.

NIGHTMARE FACTS

1. Some orb-weaver species make sticky globes out of their silk. They put a smell on them to attract certain insects. They dangle the globes from lines of thread and reel them in when bugs get stuck!

2. The largest species of orb weaver lives in Madagascar. It can grow to be 4.7 inches (12 cm) long!

3. Some orb weavers build their orb webs at about a person's head level along woodland trails. Hikers may be in for a sticky surprise as they walk!

4. The Cyclosa orb weaver makes a line of its old, shed skin and dead bug parts along one of the sticky threads in its web. It then hides in this line, looking like another piece of stuff stuck in the web.

5. Black and yellow Argiope spiders, a kind of orb weaver, can be up to 3 inches (8 cm) long. These spiders can eat bats!

6. Darwin's bark spiders make a silk that is 10 times stronger than the material used in bulletproof vests. These spiders also make the largest of all spider webs.

LONELY IN THE WEB

Most species of orb weavers are **solitary**. This means they live alone and come together only when it is time to mate. One **genus** of orb-weaver spiders does live in groups, though. This genus is called Metepeira. These orb weavers make large common webs, which they live in together.

Male furrow spiders, a type of orb weaver, live with the females during mating time. Because their eyesight is poor, they use their sense of touch to communicate. They do this by shaking the web in certain patterns.

These furrow spiders are living together because it is mating time. Females can lay up to three egg sacs at a time, each with as many as 1,400 eggs in it!

GOT YOU!

Orb weavers do not hunt for **prey**. The orb weaver spins its web with sticky threads made to catch flying insects. These strong threads keep the insect from breaking free while the spider goes to where the prey is stuck. Orb weavers use their feet to walk along the threads that are not sticky. When they reach their prey, they bite it and wrap it in silk.

Orb weavers do not actively hunt. Instead, they wait for prey to get caught in their webs. They must be ready to wrap caught prey in silk before they can get away.

Like other spiders, orb weavers put chemicals in the insect to turn the insect's insides into **liquid**. Then they suck up the juice. Orb weavers usually prey on flies, moths, beetles, wasps, bees, mosquitoes, and any other insects that fly into the web and get trapped.

BABY ORB WEAVERS

When it is time to mate, orb-weaving males will look for a female's web. In fact, they spend much of their lives wandering around, looking for a female to mate with. The female may use special chemicals that have a smell to tell males she is available and old enough to mate. The male will **vibrate** the web in a certain pattern to let the female know he is there and is not just an insect caught in the web.

These male and female orb weavers are ready to mate. The female is the larger one.

The female lays 100 or more eggs in a silken egg sac. When the spiderlings, or baby spiders, hatch, they look just like small versions of the adults. They can spin a perfect web from the day they hatch.

A female orb-weaver spider has laid an egg sac in her web. Female orb-weavers usually die before their babies are born.

These orb-weaver spiderlings have just hatched. Their web is on a plant called an obedient plant.

19

WATCH OUT, ORB WEAVER!

Spiders are hunters and eat countless insects each year. However, they are also on the menu for many animals. Birds, frogs, larger insects, monkeys, and other spiders are all possible **predators** to orb weavers.

To stay safe, most orb weavers hide or stay very still during the day. They come out at night to fix their webs and eat.

One of the animals that eats orb-weaver spiders is the praying mantis. Praying mantises hold on to their prey with their front legs.

This orb-weaver spider is using camouflage to avoid predators. Can you see the orb-weaver spider?

Some orb weavers are **camouflaged**, or colored to blend with their surroundings. Camouflage works to help the spider in two ways. First, it makes it hard for predators to see them. Camouflage also helps orb weavers sneak up on prey that they want to eat without being easily seen.

ORB-WEAVER SPIDERS AND PEOPLE

Orb-weaver spiders often live near people. However, they are not dangerous. These spiders are not **aggressive**. Their **venom**, or poison, is not **toxic** to people, either. These spiders are helpful to people, too. They eat many pest insects, such as mosquitoes, that carry diseases and beetles and other insects that damage crops.

If you find an orb-weaver web, do not tear it down. Leave it there for others to see and enjoy.

Orb-weaver spiders can live near people as long as people do not disturb their homes. There are about 180 species of orb weavers living in North America.

GLOSSARY

abdomen (AB-duh-mun) The large, rear part of an insect's body.

aggressive (uh-GREH-siv) Ready to fight.

arachnids (uh-RAK-nidz) A type of animal that includes spiders and ticks.

camouflaged (KA-muh-flahjd) Hidden by looking like the things around something.

genus (JEE-nus) The scientific name for a group of plants or animals that are alike.

liquid (LIH-kwed) Matter that flows.

mating (MAYT-ing) Coming together to make babies.

orb (ORB) A sphere or globe.

pedipalps (PEH-duh-palps) Appendages on arachnids.

predators (PREH-duh-terz) Animals that kill other animals for food.

prey (PRAY) An animal that is hunted by another animal for food.

solitary (SAH-leh-ter-ee) Spending most time alone.

species (SPEE-sheez) One kind of living thing. All people are one species.

spinnerets (spih-nuh-RETS) Parts, located on the rear of the spider's body, that make silk.

toxic (TOK-sik) Poisonous.

venom (VEH-num) A poison passed by one animal into another through a bite or a sting.

vibrate (VY-brayt) To move back and forth quickly.

INDEX

WEBSITES

Due to the changing nature of Internet links, PowerKids Press has developed an online list of websites related to the subject of this book. This site is updated regularly. Please use this link to access the list: www.powerkidslinks.com/ncs/orb/